Healing thru words

Sharissa Garcia

Presentation by *BookLeaf Publishing*

Web: www.bookleafpub.com

E-mail: info@bookleafpub.com

ISBN: 9789357617680

First edition 2022

PREFACE

I've often found that writing is therapeutic as I continue to heal. Speaking it out loud can be intimidating, and overwhelming, so I turn to written word. At least this way, I won't stumble and trip over my words. I hope that my words can provide comfort, encouragement or maybe inspire others to share their story. Although we may feel alone and in the depths of despair do we tend to believe that we are, but the truth is, we're not alone.

No More Silence

No more silence
I will not let my anxious thoughts silence my
voice.
I will not keep my mouth shut in fear of
judgement, in fear of being called names
Each time I hold back from saying what I really
want to say, apart of me dies inside.
My heart aches
No more silence
I vow to always speak up and voice my opinion
I vow to fight back against the stigma of those
who struggle with a mental illness.
No more silence
I am not my diagnosis
I am not crazy, or attention seeking for saying
how I feel
You will not deter me from making my voice
known.
No more silence
I choose to share my struggles, not for sympathy
but hopefully to inspire
I choose to speak my truth fearlessly in the face
of criticism
I choose to be a listening ear and an ally for
those who are struggling

I choose to turn my weaknesses into strengths
No more silence
I hope that these words provide comfort
I hope that we normalize that it's okay to
struggle
I hope that you find your voice
No more silence
I will not drown in my thoughts
I will not falter
I will not fear everything and run
Instead I will face everything and rise
No more silence

Let go/Hold on

And so it begins
The silence takes over
The darkness creeps in
I'm fighting for closure

Trying to let go

My mind likes to play tricks on me
It makes me feel weak and overwhelmed
I wish that I could just be free
Ripping apart at the seams, unhemmed

Trying to hold on

The tears fall freely from eyes
The pain in my chest tightens
I wish that someone would hear my cries
Sitting alone in the dark and frightened

Trying to let go

My mind and my thoughts consumed by you
I wish it wasn't this way
I wish you knew
All that I still have yet to say

Trying to hold on

I am not sure that I have the strength
It's unbearable to have you close but yet so far
For you, I'd go to great lengths
I fell in love with who you are

Trying to let go

But it seems we could never be
Too many obstacles in the way
I wish that it could be you and me
I'm still unsure if I should stay

Trying to hold on

I feel like I lost a piece of me
Trying to prove my worth to you
If only you could see
Somehow I know I'll make it through

Trying to let go

I'm trying to let go but hold on
But the more I hold on
I know I must let go

Messy

No one ever talks about how messy healing is
They just state the positive benefits, once it's over
As if healing is a one time thing but rather a lifetime
But putting in the work is what makes the journey to the destination rough

Rough is an understatement
Healing is
Twists and turns
Peaks and valleys
Hills and mountains

You'll wonder if it will ever get better
Two steps forward, 10 steps back
Small leap forward, big set back
It's like you're doing the salsa

There will be good days
Bad days
Okay days
Rough days
You'll think you've healed
But you have not, it's not over
Keep going

Trust the process

Days you'll want to throw in the towel and quit
Nights you'll cry yourself to sleep wondering if
the pain will get easier
Your mind will not be kind
It'll feel overwhelming, unbearable, unbeatable
You'll contemplate suicide
You'll think its easier that way
You'll be drained of your energy
Life just doesn't seem worth it anymore
But you still hold on

There will be times, you won't shower for days
You'll stay in bed
Barely eating
Barely breathing
Questioning why you exist, why you're
struggling, what you did to deserve this pain
You'll question if you're cared about, loved,
worthy
Fighting ugly thoughts
Fighting inner demons
Don't let them win

In the end it'll be okay
This is healing they don't talk about
It's not pretty
It's messy

Sometimes

Sometimes, I sit alone in my room
Feeling worthless, hopeless and alone
I feel this impending doom
And I slip further into the unknown

Sometimes, I think there's got to be an easier
way
I wish I understood why I deserved the things I
had happen to me
No matter how bad things got, I stayed
Crippling anxiety, depression, disassociation,
self doubt and I'm just longing to be free

The darkness comes creeping in
Unwanted thoughts plague me
This can't be how it's always been

I'm not my thoughts
I know they're not true
But this is what I'll report
Feeling so much is lost

Flashbacks, disassociation, depersonalization,
nightmares

Feeling unsafe, and questioning what's real
around me
I wipe my own tears
This is not something you'd want to see

Sometimes, the pain is too much to bear
How do I stop myself from feeling all this
I'd rather be anywhere but here
I slip further into dark abyss

I wish

I wish that I were over you
But yet, you're still on my mind
Every day, every hour, every minute

I wish that I hadn't met you
Then I wouldn't wonder
If maybe someday we could be

The chemistry, the laughs, the jokes
Caring, helpful, thoughtful
All made me fall

I knew you weren't ready
And deep down, I'm not either
But I'd be willing to try for you

Sometimes, I think I'm just not enough
You couldn't be with someone like me
Then sometimes I think, that can't be

Despite my flaws, my insecurities
I'm a catch
I'm worth it.

I still wish for the impossible

Deep down, I know that it won't be
It's too bad

I wish I were over you
And I'm not
I don't know when that day will be.

More than

Sometimes, I think you were too busy noticing
my flaws
All the while, I was overlooking yours and
accepting
I'm more than the version you've made up of me
in our head

Demons

Abuse after abuse
Pain after pain
Heartache after heartache

I was conditioned to believe that no one could
ever love me
I was conditioned to believe that I was crazy
I was conditioned to believe that I would never
be worth anything

I was made to believe that I was ugly
I was made to believe that I was fat
I was made to believe that I was dumb
I was made to believe that I was never going to
amount to anything

Mental, emotional, verbal, sexual and physical
abuse
The pain is sometimes so prominent
My heart yearns to feel whole
Surely I can't be all that my abusers made me to
believe

These inner demons of insecurity, jealously,
anxiety

Low self-esteem, poor boundaries, people
pleasing, no confidence in who I am
These all eat away at me
Keep people at arms length and push em' away

Unlearning all that I was made to believe about
myself
Trust the process
That's what they say
But it's gruesome

I do my best
Far from perfect
Someday, it will pay off

Demons are not who I am
They are apart of me
And instead of fighting them, I'll learn to make
peace

Together, rolled into one

14

I'll overthink, I'll over love and I'll care too much
My strengths and my weaknesses
Together, rolled into one

I'll worry, I'll stress, I'll need reassurance
My inner demons may come out to play
My strengths and my weaknesses
Together, rolled into one

I'll have good days
I'll have bad days
I'll cry, I'll have sleepless nights
My strengths and my weaknesses
Together, rolled into one

Flashback/Disassociation

Flashback/Disassociation

Unexpected, sudden, frightening
I see the little girl who sat in the corner of her
dark room
Wishing there was something she could do to
forget her emotional pain
Trying to drown out the noise

Crying
Shaking
Trembling
A blade in one hand

I try to reach out to her
I scream and I yell don't do it
She doesn't hear me

She pushes the blade to her skin
I feel her pain
I know why in that instance she cut
To focus on physical pain rather than emotional
To bring her back to present day

I wish that I could hold her and let her know it's
all going to be okay
That she's strong
That she's not what her abusers have made her
out to be

Suddenly, I'm not in a dark room
The tv is playing
And I'm sitting there with tears streaming down
my face
Bewildered at what transpired
Confused as to the trigger

My heart is beating rapidly
My breaths shallow
I'm disoriented and confused
Reminding myself that I am safe

I look at my wrists
I look at my legs
There are no marks
Maybe some scars from long ago

She reorients herself to present day
My breathing calms,
I check my pulse
I'm no longer sweating
I check my surroundings
I am safe

Unspoken words

17

There's a lot that's been weighing on my mind
In my chest

These words I want to say
I'm just not sure how to

For now, I'll write and bottle it up inside me
Nothing feels heavier than these unspoken
words

Hope

I hope someday I'll find
What quiets my restless soul
And gives me piece of mind
Then, I'll fully be in control

I hope that in my darkest days
I'll still keep chasing sunsets
Finding beauty in every possible way
And everything just makes sense

I hope I'll keep chasing adventures
Learning, growing, evolving
These are life essentials
Relaxing, unwinding, becoming

I hope to always surround myself
With those who appreciate a big heart
Isn't selfish with themselves
Wisdom and knowledge, I hope to impart

Darling

Darling,

Remember you'll never be too much for the right
person
Who sees the stars in your eyes
Who accepts you wholeheartedly
No lies, no games
Whose not hot and cold

Please,
Darling
Remember you're worthy
Of all that you seek and desire
It's coming your way, be patient

Wild heart

You cannot tame her wild heart
Not even from the start

She'll wander to far off lands
See, her wings expand

Travel with her or let her go
But don't interrupt her flow

She's chaos and she's peace
Travel is her release

Don't bother, pressing restart
You can't tame her wild heart

I'm not

I'm not everyone's cup of tea
Nor do I long to be

Support me, accept all of me
Or leave me be

I'm not someone you meet twice
Here's my advise

Don't let me get away
You'll forever regret that day

Heart and Mind

22

My heart wants one thing
My mind wants another

My heart says stay
My heart says go

My heart says speak up more and don't be afraid
My mind screams be afraid and don't bother

My heart and my mind
Never in sync
Always at odds

Living with Fibromyalgia

Things are not the way it was before
I can't even remember much anymore
It's not the pain that will surely be there
It's the not knowing where

Some days you'll think the pain is gone
But when you least expect it, the pain respawns
You'll want to isolate in alone in your room
Thinking this is it, your life is just full of gloom

People will think you're faking your symptoms
But they don't understand a fucked up central
nervous system
Doing little tasks aren't easy
And sometimes the thought of so much to do
makes you queasy

Chronic illness/pain is no joke
Be kind to us folk
We never asked for any of this
Our old selves we really do miss

We get up everyday
Knowing the pain will be there anyway
But if we rest we'll be called lazy

Our memories will also be hazy

Two hundred plus symptoms that can attack
Trust me, I know, it's a lot to unpack
Try living a day in my shoes
Maybe it will give you a different point of view

Sometimes there won't be much that we can do
But to just make it through
We're warriors and we're strong
We live with fibromyalgia, we just keep moving
along

Could've been

I've often wondered if it's possible to fall in love
with someone you never dated
And I've discovered that you can
How long you've known someone means
nothing
But rather how this person makes you feel
overtime

I'm still wondering how to get over someone you
were never with
I'll always wonder what could've been
It's like trying to tell the story of a book I've
never read
Sometimes I wish we had met under different
circumstances.

My fear is that even years from now
I'll see your face
I'll see your smile
You'll ask me how I've been
And I'll smile and keep it casual
But you won't see my heart skip a beat.
You won't see me trying to catch my breath

On the outside looking in,

I'll look fine
But deep down,
I want to scream from the rooftops, just give us a
chance

True Strength

Often we think true strength is keeping it within
ourselves
And this couldn't be further from the truth

Don't be afraid to feel sad, to feel angry, to feel
despair, to feel hopeless, to feel powerless
We've all been there

But don't let those feelings fester for too long
inside you
Recognize them, process them and then when
you're ready, release them

Let them go
Welcome in love, hope, joy, peace, calm and
clarity

There is a beauty in vulnerability
Speak your truth, own it, and live it

Be you

28

Be you
And just, who is that?

Be quirky, be weird
Follow your dreams, follow your passion

Cry if you must, laugh a little longer
They may call you crazy

So what?
Live your life anyway

Be you
Be unapologetically you

That's not me

When my inner demons come out to play
It's not the prettiest sight
I try with all my might
To not let it push you away

But I hope that you know
That's not me, deep down to my core
I hope that you're not keeping score
I'm trying to go with the flow

I've never been able to trust
Skillfully manipulated and undermined
Fooling my heart, playing with my mind
I know this has all been discussed

I ask that you be patient with me
Don't let my inner demons be a red flag
It can be a drag
But I know that's not me, guarantee

I hope that there will come a day

And I hope that there will come a day
When you won't have to choke back what you
want to say
And I hope that there will come a day
When you aren't having to keep your feelings at
bay

And I hope that there will come a day
When you won't have to prove your worth to a
man
And I hope that there will come a day
When you won't be treated less than

And I hope that there will come a day
When you're ailments and pains are non-existent
And I hope that there will come a day
When you'll find someone consistent, and not
distant

And I hope that there will come a day
When all your hopes, and dreams come true
And I hope that there will come a day
When you can sit back and enjoy a beautiful
view

9 789357 617680